*Ellie Bedford*

# Paphos

*The Paphos hillside at sunset*

## Paphos 3-Day Itinerary: Live like a local!

By Ellie Bedford

**Address:**

Unanchor Press
P.O. Box 184
Durham, NC 27701
www.unanchor.com

**Ordering Information:**

Quantity sales. Special discounts are available on quantity purchases by corporations, associations, and others. For details, contact the publisher at the address above.

Orders by U.S. trade bookstores and wholesalers. Please contact Unanchor at hello@unanchor.com, or visit http://www.unanchor.com.

*Printed in the United States of America*

*Unanchor is a global family for travellers to experience the world with the heart of a local.*

**UNANCHOR**

# Table of Contents

# Introduction

=============

IMPORTANT INFORMATION FOR TRAVELLERS TO PAPHOS

Paphos has excitedly been awarded the 2017 European Capital of Culture! Whilst this is great news, it should be noted that as a result of certain guidelines, there is currently a great deal of construction work on the roads in central Paphos.

I encourage everyone to not let this put you off visiting our amazing island but I would advise visitors that some of the directions and parking information within my guide (and others alike) may be somewhat disrupted as a result.

I will, of course, update the guide alongside any permanent changes to our town. Thank you!

Your very own extensive guide to how to live like a local in Paphos, this itinerary allows you to discover places enjoyed by locals but usually ignored by guide books. After all, when visiting somewhere, the best places are found by following the locals!

A lot of the tourists who come to this beautiful island miss out on the best parts due to being glued to their sunbeds. If you want to mix it up a bit, visit traditional villages and sample some of the best local food on offer then this itinerary is for you!

With all the research already completed for you, all you need to do is concentrate on enjoying everything that Paphos has to offer.

**Benefit from insider tips and useful information such as:**

- *Transportation information*
- *Directions to car parks (all of which are free!)*
- *Advice on local food*
- *Nightlife recommendations*
- *Useful local phrases*
- *Over 50 extremely detailed and annotated maps (no danger of getting lost!)*
- *Estimated fuel costs for each journey*
- *Climate information and tips on what to expect from the different seasons*
- *Cultural hotspots and day trip advice*
- *My contact details should you need any further information*

**Activities within the itinerary**

- *Discover the local village of Lysos on horseback*
- *The best local food and drink experiences from trendy cafes to local tavernas*
- *Visit to Paphos Zoo*
- *Extremely detailed walking tours of Kato Paphos and Polis*
- *Winery visit*

**Who is this itinerary for?**

- *Travelers who want to avoid the tourist traps*
- *People who want a cultural alternative to museums*
- *Couples/groups of friends/families - it really is suitable for all (even at the winery there are lots of things for kids to see and do!)*
- *Anyone who loves food!*
- *Individuals who want a mixture of relaxation and adventure*

(Please note, I would recommend hiring a rental car, especially for day 3, as it will work out cheaper and more convenient. I have included details of where and how to do so in the appendix.)

**I love being able to call this island my home and my aim is to make travelers see what I see as a local.**

**So, get ready to discover the heart and soul of Cyprus!**

# Day 1

=============

## 9:30 am -- Deck Cafe - Breakfast

- **Price:** EUR €15.00 (for a single adult)
- **Duration:** 1 hour
- **Address:** Poseidonos Avenue, Kato Pafos

A wonderful spot to start off your day, Deck Cafe offers a great variety of breakfast deals as well as fresh coffee and juices. Situated along the main harbour road, just far enough away from the hustle and bustle, here you can enjoy breath-taking views of the coast.

The staff are wonderfully friendly and you can benefit from the free wifi on offer. The whole establishment is rather stylish; from the outside, canopied area with its palm tree lined pathway below, to the quirky presentation of the food. Even the bill arrives in a sleek little envelope with complimentary sweets.

Should you have little ones to think of, the cafe has a toy box to keep them occupied!

The prices are fairly reasonable; however, some items may seem a little less value for money (for example, fresh juice is €4.60). Having said that, on average you should be looking to pay around €10-15 per person and I find this to be a very good deal considering the atmosphere, service and quality of food.

**Local Tip:** *Try a 'Cypriot coffee'! This is how the locals start off their mornings. Served in a small cup, this coffee is intense in flavour (similar to espresso). Order 'Sketo' if you'd prefer black, 'Metrio' if you'd like one sugar and 'Gliko' for two sugars.*

In the summer, relax outside on the beautiful decking under the parasols and even take a swim in the sea before getting changed in the nearby changing rooms (charge of 50 cents). If visiting in the winter, although the outside area is closed in, the view is still spectacular and you can cuddle up by the open fire. No matter the season, enjoy an after breakfast stroll on the beach.

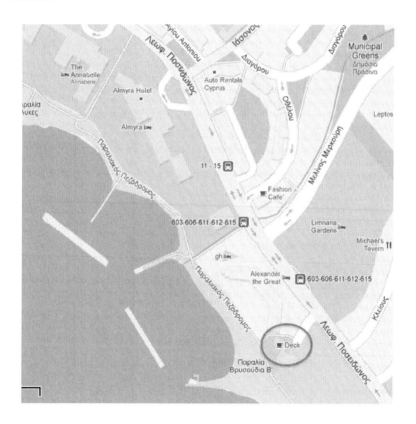

## 10:30 am -- Walking Tour of Kato Paphos

- **Price:** FREE
- **Duration:** 1 hour and 30 minutes
- **Address:** Deck Cafe to Paphos Castle

This is a rather scenic stroll, offering a bit of history without any trips to musty museums and all the attractions are free! The duration of the tour will depend on how long you want to spend admiring all the wonderful culture!

## PART 1

Starting off from Deck Cafe, head towards the sea and turn right. This is one path; all you need to do is follow the coast! You'll have the opportunity to take advantage of the beautiful coastline and beaches in this area as you meander through the palm tree lined pathways.

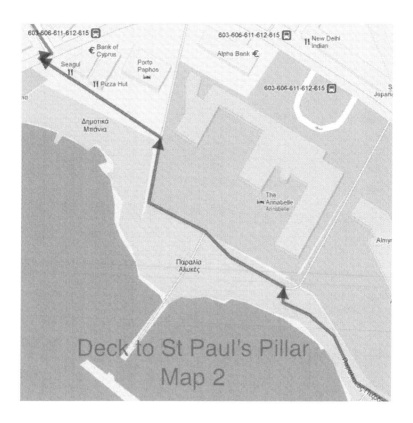

You'll pass a few of the major hotels on your right. Look out for The Alexander the Great Beach, Almyra and Annabelle hotels and once you have passed all these you'll see a small fork in the pathway. Keep left, passing Pizza Hut and the Seagull restaurants on your right.

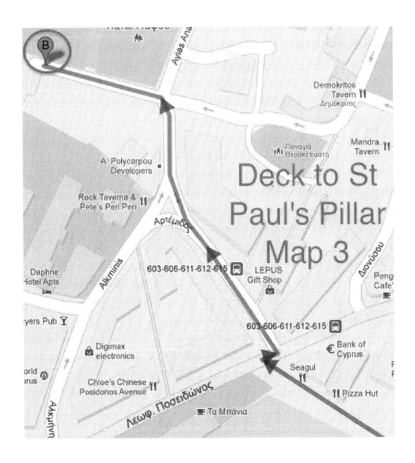

Here you will meet the main road. Cross over, you should see a bank on your left and Tea for Two restaurant on your right. A little further down the road you will come to a fork in the road where you should keep to the right. When you come to the crossroads (of sorts!) take a left. At the end of this road you will find the Ayia Kyriaki Church.

## St Paul's Pillar

Located within the church grounds you will find St Paul's Pillar. St Paul was allegedly tied to this pillar and lashed for preaching Christianity in 45 A.D, which was against the beliefs of the Roman general in command at the time.

The church itself is currently used as the Anglican church of Paphos and was built in the 13th Century. Some of the original mosaics on the floors of the church have still been preserved.

## PART 2

Head back down the road you came up and at the crossroads you came across before, take a left. Carry on down this road until you meet a mini roundabout. This is the beginning of bar street (for future reference). This area may seem rather garishly

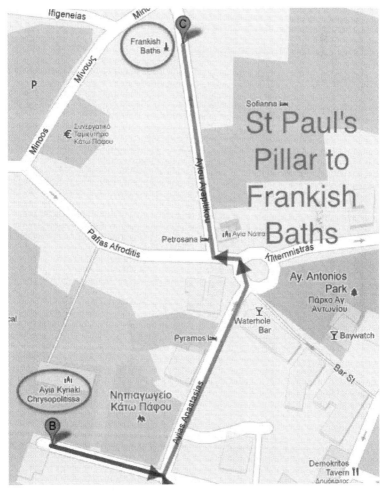

touristic but fear not, there is much culture to be discovered!

Cross over the roundabout, walk to your left and then take the immediate road to your right. Continue down this road until you see the signs for the Frankish Baths on your left.

**Frankish Baths**

Once a public bathing house, the Frankish Baths were originally constructed at the end of the 14th century. It was rebuilt during the Ottoman period with some of the domed roofs being replaced with cupolas. I particularly enjoyed the old tree growing out of one of the ceilings!

## PART 3

Coming out of the Baths, turn left and at the crossroads take a right. Follow this road until it ends and then turn right. Continue down this road and take your first left. Heading up this road towards the main road, the church is on your left by the traffic lights.

Frankish Baths to Agioi Anargyroi Church

## Agioi Anargyroi Church

A relatively new church, The construction of the temple began
in 1980 while the inauguration took place in July 1994. It is just
fabulously beautiful and a great example of the Greek
Orthodox religion. It was built as a result of the number of
Greek Orthodox worshippers becoming overwhelming for such
a small city. Magnificent icons and elaborate light fixtures make
this a magical place to see and it is often overlooked by tourists
in favour of older, more historical buildings. My favourite part
of this extraordinary building is the colourful and modern
stained glass windows!

## PART 4

When walking out of the main entrance of the church, follow
the main road to your left until you see a crossroads with traffic
lights and take another left. Continue down this road until you
see a bus stop on your right. The entrance to the Catacomb
should be on your left.

### Agia Solomoni Catacomb

Saint Solomoni was one of the first prominent figures to adopt
Christianity in Cyprus, refusing to succumb to the idolatry of
the Roman times. Her beliefs are said to have led her into
hiding within the walls of the caves to escape persecution.
According to historical legend, the Romans, on discovering
Solomoni's refuge, walled up the entrance to the caves.
However, when they came to open the entrance 200 years
later, the saint walked out alive.

Nowadays, there is a marvelous tree outside the catacomb which is said to have healing properties. Locals tie pieces of cloth as offerings to the Saint.

The catacomb is a world heritage site and the caves themselves, lead out into ancient mosaics above. From here you can take advantage of the fantastic views of Paphos. Within the catacomb, there is a shrine to Solomoni and there are remains of Christian Orthodox wall paintings dating back to the 12th Century.

## PART 5

Turning left as you come out of the catacomb entrance, walk along this main road. You should eventually see a car park to your right. This is also where the main bus station is situated. After the large bus station on the right, keep walking, cross the road and turn right so you are walking along the harbour front towards the castle.

This is where most of the good seafood restaurants are in Kato Paphos! Walk through all the kiosks and cafes (beware of the waiters, they will try their best to entice you!) and at the end of the strip, before you hit the castle, you will find Hobo Cafe.

After all the walking and exploring you'll need a bit of a rest! Use this lovely local haunt to recharge your batteries and look out for the Pelican!

*Hobo Cafe, a waterside relaxation spot*

## 12:00 pm -- Hobo Cafe - Lunch

- **Price:** EUR €10.00 (for a single adult)
- **Duration:** 1 hour and 30 minutes
- **Address:** 4 Apostolou Pavlou Avenue, Kato Paphos

This lovely little waterside relaxation spot offers a wonderful variety of dishes at really reasonable prices. Not only is the atmosphere fantastic but the waiters are friendly and the food is extremely tasty!

You can choose from Greek dishes such as gyropita (toasted kebab in pita), exotic seafood salads and other more continental foods such as the chicken fajitas. I would highly recommend the burgers. They come with tasty, crispy fries and there are many different varieties on offer should you wish to add bacon, cheese or egg to your burger!

There is also a great deal of exciting coffees ranging from ice cream frappes to specialty alcoholic coffee cocktails. Their smoothies and milkshakes are also great (and massive!).

*Local Tip: Whilst waiting for your meal, take a look inside the art gallery next door. Known as the 'En Plo' gallery there is usually a wonderful array of local art and crafts on display.*

Also, keep an eye out for the Pelican! He sits on the wall by the outside seating area and likes to pose for passersby!

## 1:30 pm -- Hobo Cafe to Paphos Zoo

- **Price:** EUR €3.00 (for a single adult)
- **Duration:** 25 minutes

This journey takes around 25 minutes to half an hour and is a simple drive, straight along the coast towards Peyia.

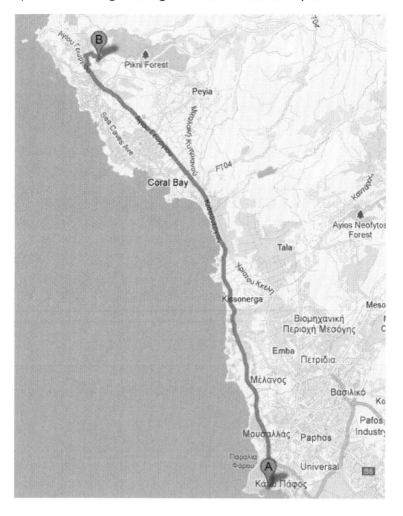

Seeing as you have just finished your walking tour, you probably won't have a car nearby. Therefore, I've given you a bit of time to organise the pick up of your hire car from the rental company or to get back to where you are staying should you have already arranged said transportation. For more information on hiring a car, visit the Appendix section of the itinerary.

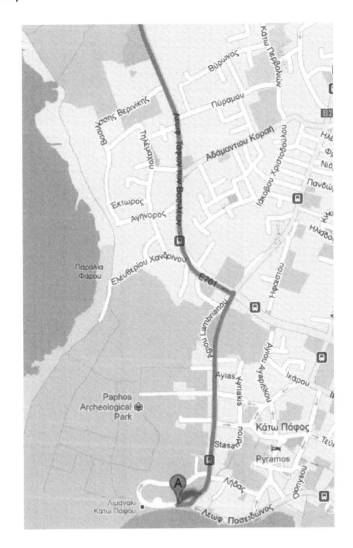

From the harbour area, head towards the center of town, when you reach the traffic lights at the crossroads by Tomb of the Kings, turn left and head towards Coral Bay. You will stay on this road for some time, passing signs for Chloraka, Kissonerga and Saint George. You will pass many coastal hotels on your left such as the Elysium Beach Resort, Venus Beach (on your left), Paradise Cove Villas, Laura Beach and Queen's Bay.

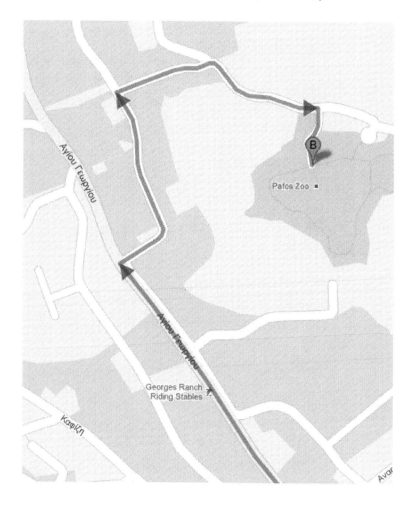

When you get to the roundabout by Coral Bay, go straight over, taking your second turning. Do the same at the next roundabout and you will pass Coral Bay Karting on your right. Keep straight for around 5km, carrying on straight when you meet the crossroads.

At some point you should pass Theanan Seaview Villas as well as George's Stables on your left. You will see signs for Paphos Zoo and take your second right after the stables. Follow the road as it bends to the left and take your first right. At the end of this road stay right and then take your next right soon after. You will see the Zoo at the end of this road.

The petrol cost for this journey is around €3.

## 2:00 pm -- Paphos Zoo

- **Price:** EUR €15.50 (for a single adult)
- **Duration:** 3 hours
- **Address:** St George, Peyeia, P.O.Box 66620, Pafos

Although very popular with tourists, the Zoo is a great day out for all and it's the number one day out for locals (especially those with children!).

Originally established as one man's (Christos Christoforou's) private wildlife collection, Paphos Zoo started as a bird park and opened in 2003 as a fully fledged zoo.

Located in St George, around a half an hour drive from central Paphos, this Zoo is steadily becoming the most popular in Cyprus and the people of Paphos are proud of the growing collection of exotic animals housed there.

At Paphos Zoo, there is more to do than simply wander around and admire the wildlife. There is an amphitheatre that hosts parrot and owl shows daily, a petting zoo for children and a museum as well as souvenir shops, an art gallery and a replica traditional Cypriot home.

During the winter season (27th October - 31st March) it is open from 9am to 5pm and during the summer months this is extended to 6pm. Adult admission is €15.50 and €8.50 for children under 13.

There are also plenty of buses running to and from the zoo should you not have the use of a car.

For more information you can contact the zoo directly on (00357) 26813852 or visit the website at www.pafoszoo.com.

Now, I've given you some time to get back from the zoo to where you are staying, wash up and head out on the town!

## 7:00 pm -- Temple Bar - Dinner and Drinks

- **Price:** EUR €15.00 (for a single adult)
- **Duration:** 4 hours and 55 minutes
- **Address:** 1st April street, Paphos

One of the most popular local hangouts in town, Temple Bar offers a wonderful mix of old-school rock and roll, alternative and soul music.

Take a seat in one of the booths or (in the warmer seasons) outside underneath the fantastic lantern-strewn tree, and take your pick from classic dishes such as pork chops and burgers or something slightly different such as king prawns (when available) or pork belly. The platters are also amazing with a variety of meats and cheeses (should you get peckish later on!). Meals are all around €10 to €15 and food is served until late.

There is a wide range of spirits behind the bar to choose from but should you fancy some wine I would recommend Vasilikon, a wonderful local dry white, served by the bottle for €18. You can also enjoy a freshly made Mojito for €8.

Inside you'll find wonderful decorations ranging from old bicycles and Native American artwork to old records and rock posters.

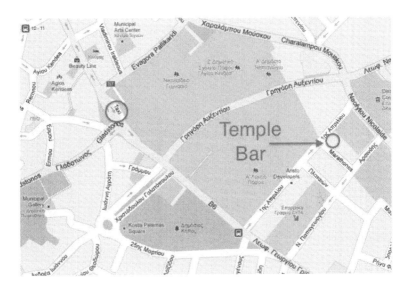

***Local Tip:*** *Temple also offers a flavoured tobacco menu and you can have your very own Hookah pipe brought to your table for €12.*

Live music nights are a frequent occurrence at Temple and usually consist of guitar players as well as DJ's. For more information on the bar, menu and events visit their facebook page here: https://www.facebook.com/TemplePub

You shouldn't need to book out of season but should you wish to plan ahead the number to call is (00357) 967 27314.

It is situated down from the main taxi rank in the city center (near the CYTA phone shop). This is one place you should not miss!

# Day 2

=============

## 10:00 am -- Atlantida Beach

- **Price:** FREE
- **Duration:** 2 hours
- **Address:** Geroskipou beach front, Paphos

Atlantida beach is situated at the beginning of Yeroskipou, the end of the major hotel area in Kato Paphos. This is where the locals go to swim, eat Kalamari and drink Frappe in the sun. There is a large grassy area for sports and games and there are often fitness and dance shows for those who wish to either observe or join in.

The public toilets leave a lot to be desired but the Fish Tavern is nice (and has its own clean toilets!) where you can enjoy a variety of seafood dishes and other Greek cuisine. Obviously, if following the itinerary, and with this being the morning, there is also a beach bar serving coffees for €3 as well as alcoholic drinks and snacks.

This is a nice place to come even in winter as the restaurant is open and the large grassy area makes it a lovely place to sit and watch the waves. Keep in mind that you are sadly not able to bring your own picnic with the restaurant grounds being in such close proximity.

### 12:00 pm -- Atlantida to Muse

- **Price:** EUR €1.00 (for a single adult)
- **Duration:** 15 minutes

As mentioned in the appendix, a hired car is something I would really recommend. If you'd rather take the bus there is a bus stop on the main road by the Luna park and they run fairly regularly (around every 20 minutes) to the center of town. See the appendix for more information on bus routes.

On leaving Atlantida, you must turn left so carry on down that road and straight over the roundabout. Carry on down the dual carriageway until you see a small triangle in the middle of the road. Here the road splits and you want to keep right.

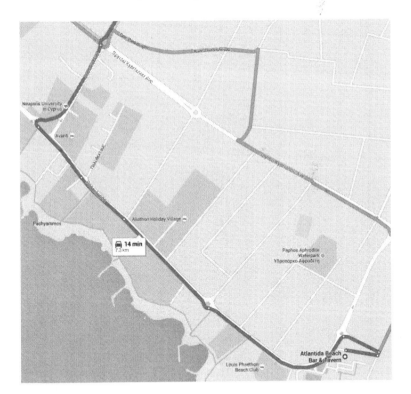

After turning right and carrying on straight you will see another roundabout and you need to go straight over, taking your second exit. Carry on down this road until you meet another roundabout by Debenhams department store then take the first exit.

Now you are heading towards the town center. The road will eventually fork slightly by the municipal gardens, at which point you need to keep left and at the roundabout take the first exit. Follow this narrow road and you will arrive at the parking area.

If you'd prefer to take a taxi, expect to pay around €10. See the appendix for useful taxi numbers.

The fuel cost for this journey is around €1.

## 12:15 pm -- Muse Cafe - Lunch

- **Price:** EUR €15.00 (for a single adult)
- **Duration:** 1 hour and 10 minutes
- **Address:** Mousallas, Paphos

Expect to be blown away! Not only are the views breath-taking but the food is beautifully prepared and displayed and extremely tasty! This is where the locals come on their lunch breaks and it's easy to see why. You can relax outside on the comfy sofas all year round thanks to the patio heaters or if you prefer there is a stunning and modern inside eating area, complete with a streamlined bar and wonderful LED coloured lights.

The staff are wonderful, polite and helpful. The coffee is fantastic as they use freshly ground Illy coffee beans and the waiters are all trained baristas. The prices are really reasonable, with most meals costing around €10 or less. The portions are massive (even the starters!) so don't expect to leave feeling hungry!

My favourite dish is the 'Rocking Salmon Baguette', priced at €8.99, which is a brown baguette with smoked salmon and avocado and is served with wonderful fried potatoes and salad. There is also a wide range of burgers and grilled dishes such as salmon and pork.

*Local Tip: Their chicken kebab is wonderful for sharing and is served with pita bread, chips and salad; even the kids will enjoy this meal!*

You probably won't need to book at lunch time as most of the workers nearby have lunch at around 1pm-2pm, so getting there early will ensure you get first pick of the seating. You may wish to come here one evening too as they have a wonderful cocktail menu and it really is a great spot for watching the sunset.

**For more information visit the website here:**
www.muse-kitchen-bar.com

**For reservations call:** (00357) 26 941 951

## 1:25 pm -- Muse to Vouni Panayias Winery

- **Price:** EUR €5.00 (for a single adult)
- **Duration:** 35 minutes

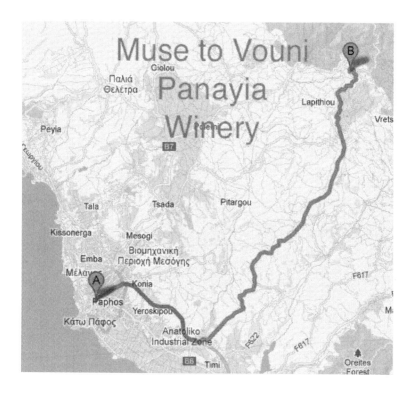

This car journey takes around 35 minutes but is a lovely drive. After a bit of motorway driving, you can discover the beauty of the vast farm lands and admire the tradition that exists just outside the hubbub of the city.

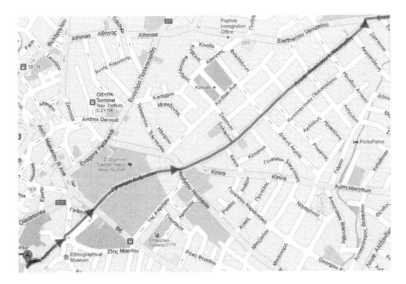

On leaving Muse, head out the same way you came in until you hit the mini roundabout then take the second exit.

Carry out straight down this road, crossing over two sets of crossroads. When you come to the end of the road take a right.

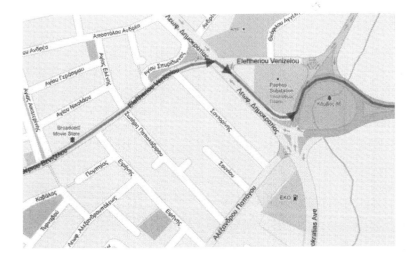

Keep going until you meet the traffic lights and then turn right.
Continue towards the roundabout and take your second exit
onto the A6 (towards Limassol).

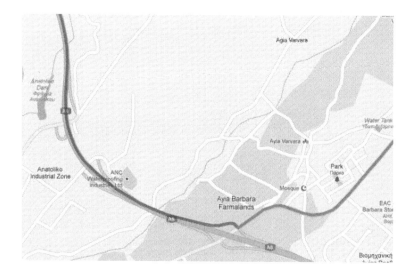

After around 7km, take the exit on your right, signposted E606,
and then at the end of the slip road, turn left onto the E606.
You will continue on this road for around 20km.

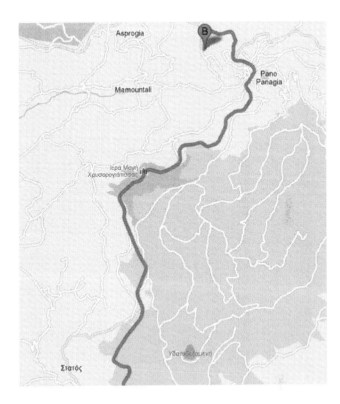

Eventually you will come to a stadium on your right. Take a left here and carry on straight for around another 6km.

It's a rather windy road but after passing the Chrysoroyiatissa Monastery (a bit of a mouthful, I know!) on your left you should find the winery situated on a sharp bend on your left.

The fuel cost for this journey is around €5.

# 2:00 pm -- Vouni Panayia Winery

- **Price:** EUR €5.00 (for a single adult)
- **Duration:** 3 hours
- **Address:** Vouni Panayia Winery, E703, Pano Panagia,

Escaping the noise of the city for a while, it's time for some indulgence. Cyprus is known for its farm land, orchards and vineyards, and the Mediterranean climate is beautifully accommodating for many grape varieties.

The village of Panayia is alive with history. This is where the legendary president Makarios was born and raised, who played a vital role in securing independence for Cyprus after almost a century of British rule. If time is on your side, take a wander around the village and visit the museum dedicated to Makarios.

A family owned and run winery, Vouni Panayia was founded over 25 years ago by Andreas Kyriakides and his wife Thelma. Their passion and spirit is still evident throughout the vineyard today and their dedication has led to their wines being some of the most recognized in Cyprus.

Enjoy a guided tour of the winery and even a spot of wine and cheese tasting to round off your day! The tour costs €5, lasts approximately 45 minutes and it is necessary to book in advance (see contact details below).

There is more than just wine on offer too! Visitors can see how grape juice is made to create other Cypriot delicacies such as Soutjouko (pronounced in Cypriot 'Shoushouko') which are a combination of nuts and flour that have been sun-dried.

**Local Tip:** *Do not miss out on the dry red wine known as 'Barba-Yiannis'. It is made from the highest quality local 'Maratheftiko' variety, which is cultivated in the mountainous regions of Paphos. It also won Bronze at the international wine festival in Thessaloniki in 2003.*

The winery is open daily from 10am to 5pm.

**Tel:** (00357) 26 722 770 or (00357) 99 453 138

**Email:** info@vounipanayiawinery.com

**Website:** www.vounipanayiawinery.com

Now I've allowed a bit of time between the winery activity and dinner so that you can get back to wherever you are staying and get ready...

In case you are unsure on your way back I've also included a map with directions back to Kato Paphos:

Turn right onto the road you came in on and follow it round to the right. Pass the monastery on your right and turn right at the stadium.

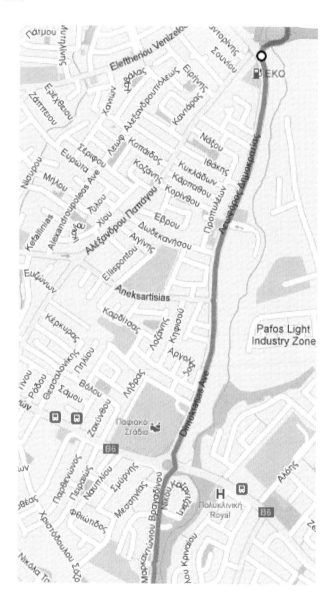

Keep straight, following signs for the A6. Leave the E606 and turn right onto the A6. Carry on until you meet the large roundabout. You are now back in Paphos town! Take your first exit and carry on straight on the dual carriageway and you will meet another roundabout. Go straight over and continue straight at the next set of traffic lights.

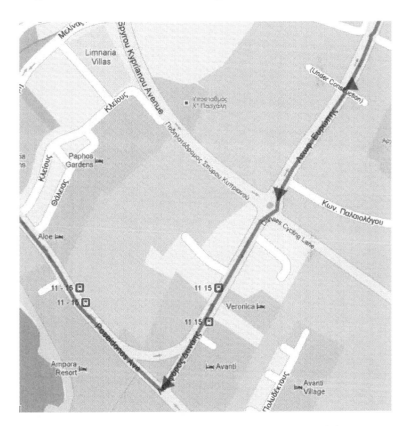

When you meet the next small roundabout, go straight over again, passing the 'Veronica' hotel on your left and take a right at the end of the road. If you follow this road that runs parallel to the coast, you will eventually meet the harbour.

## 7:20 pm -- Kato Paphos to Myrra Taverna

- **Price:** EUR €0.50 (for a single adult)
- **Duration:** 10 minutes

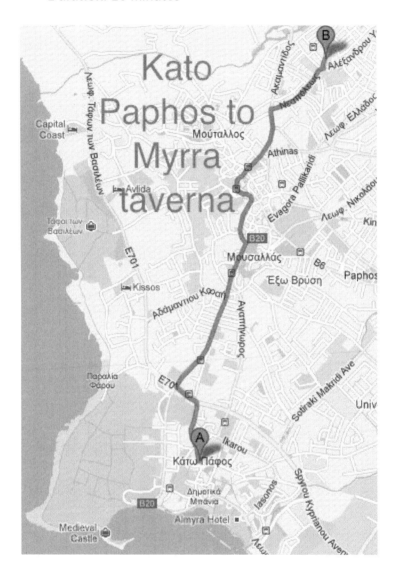

After getting back from the winery, it will probably be time to head back to the hotel/apartment, have a rest and get your glad rags on! The next part of our local journey is a visit to a taverna, a must for any visitor to Cyprus! These directions are from Kato Paphos as this is a good starting point seeing as this will more than likely be where you are staying.

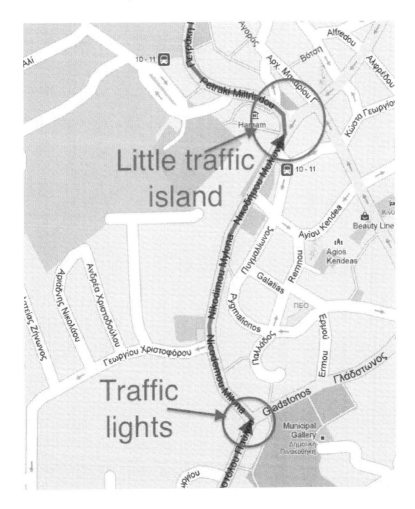

After following the main road over the crossroads/traffic lights by Begonia garden center, carry on up towards the town center. When you reach the crossroads at the fork in the road, keep to the left. Follow the road round to the left and at the little island keep left again.

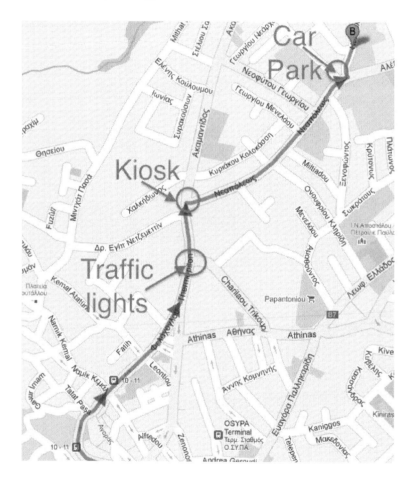

Follow the road round to the right and keep straight, the road will branch to the left slightly. Go straight over the traffic lights and take your next right at the kiosk. Carry on down this road, taking the 4th road on your left and the car park area is directly on your left. Myrra Taverna is situated on the opposite side of the road.

The fuel cost for this journey is around 50 cents.

# 7:30 pm -- Myrra Taverna - Dinner

- **Price:** EUR €20.00 (for a single adult)
- **Duration:** 2 hours and 25 minutes
- **Address:** 37 Neapoleos Street, Paphos

A little secret gem in the heart of Paphos old town, Myrra Taverna represents everything that a Cypriot dinner should be! Family run and overwhelmingly welcoming, this little restaurant is unobtrusive but extraordinary at the same time.

*Local Tip:* Order the meze! A beautiful selection of small dishes, the meze is the perfect way to sample lots of different types of local cuisine (see the appendix for more information on mezes). Myrra is the only taverna in the area that offers prawns with its meat meze!

The seating area outside is beautiful with a hubbub of local activity in the warmer months. If visiting in the winter months, the inside is just as lovely with its wide variety of traditional decorations and quaint layout.

Meals will cost you no more than €20 a head including wine. Here, they grow almost all of their own vegetables and the dishes are freshly prepared that day (no need for freezers here!). The service is brilliant and, with it being a family run restaurant, you can tell that the staff put their heart and soul into the taverna. If you want to learn more about the dishes or, indeed, anything else about Cyprus, this lovely family, headed by Andreas, will be happy to help.

I would recommend booking in advance as it becomes busier over the weekends and later on in the evenings (Cypriots traditionally eat late).

**Tel:** (00357) 26 938 381

## 9:55 pm -- Myrra Taverna to Deloubak

- **Price:** EUR €0.50 (for a single adult)
- **Duration:** 5 minutes

I know it's been a long day but to help you round if off in style, I recommend heading back into town to the trendy and very local coffee shop (alcohol available!) Deloubak.

On leaving the restaurant, go back dowen the way you came up and carry on down Neapoleos Road until the road ends. Take a left and head into the old town. It's important to note that a lot of these side roads are one-way and can be confusing, so do be careful not to take the wrong one.

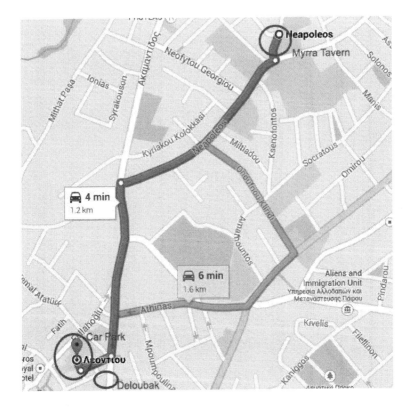

There is a very large car park (free in the evenings) within walking distance of the coffee shop. Take your next available right onto Ippocratous road and follow the signs for the car park.

Deloubak is the big coffee shop on the corner off the main road.

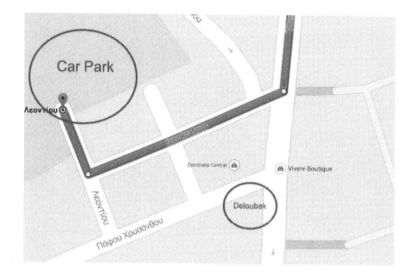

# 10:00 pm -- Deloubak Coffee Shop

- **Price:** EUR €5.00 (for a single adult)
- **Duration:** 1 hour
- **Address:** Thermopylon Road, Paphos

Deloubak opened its doors in March 2015 and is a breath of fresh air to Paphos main town. Recently, due to the economy and also the opening of the Kings Avenue Mall, a lot of the shops in the old town have been forced to close their doors. As sad as this is, local service industry business owners are starting to move into this area of Paphos and re-vamp its reputation. Coffee shops and bars are starting to spring up where there were once masses of leather shoe shops and jewellery stores.

Regarding Deloubak in particular, the owners did not rush into opening up this friendly and stylish establishment. After months of research into coffee blends and much travelling around the world in source of great produce, these two brothers, Nico and Dino, have achieved something really great.

On first walking into the Coffee shop, what hits you is the feel of the place. With its exposed brick walls, old deli-style counters and plush vintage armchairs you almost feel like you're in a trendy side street in Manhattan.

Deloubak offers a great variety of coffees, snacks, milkshakes and other refreshments, all under €4. They are open every day until 11pm.

# Day 3

=============

### 9:45 am -- Kato Paphos to Polis
- **Price:** EUR €4.50 (for a single adult)
- **Duration:** 45 minutes

Few people realise just how vast Paphos is! It's about time to venture out and see what else this wonderful district has to offer. Next stop - Polis! Please note - Sunday may not be the best time to visit Polis as many of the attractions as well as a lot of the bars and restaurants are closed.

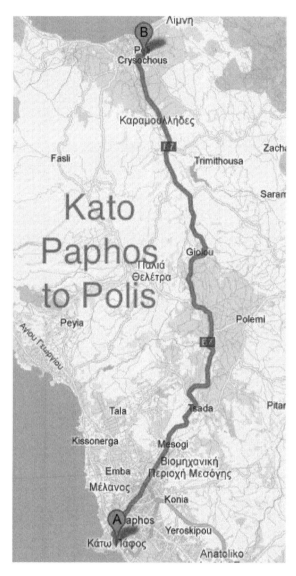

This journey is fairly simple as it is one long road (B7).

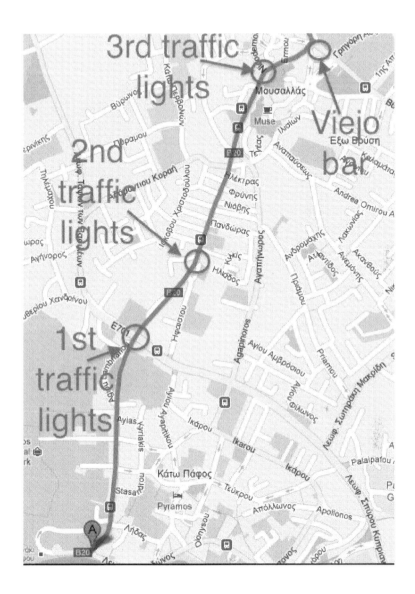

The easiest way to get onto this road is to head up from Kato Paphos over the traffic lights before the shopping area of town. When you get to Viejo on your right, turn left at the traffic lights.

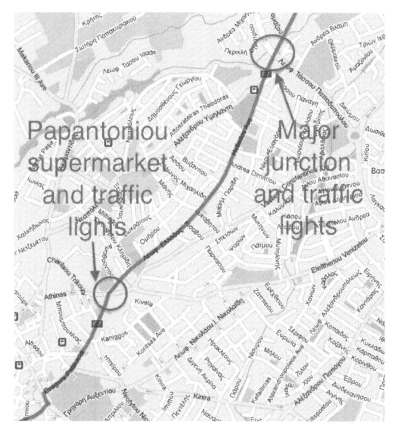

Follow this road round to the right and carry on over the traffic lights by Papantoniou supermarket.

Further on up the road you will come to a major junction (with traffic lights again!). Go straight over and you are now on what the locals call the 'Polis road'.

You will be on this road for about 33km, passing through Stoumpi, Giolou and Chrysochou.

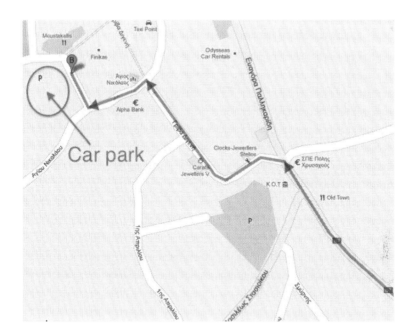

Keep straight, you should see an EKO petrol station on your left (by now, Polis should be well signposted).

On entering the old town, you must take your 2nd left, follow the road round and then turn left by Alpha Bank. Take your next right and then left and the car park should be on your left.

The fuel cost for this journey will be around €4.50.

Now it's time to explore!

## 10:30 am -- Walking Tour of Polis

- **Price:** EUR €1.70 (for a single adult)
- **Duration:** 1 hour and 30 minutes
- **Address:** Polis, Paphos,

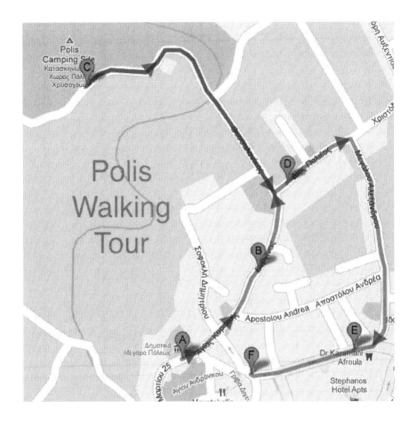

## PART 1

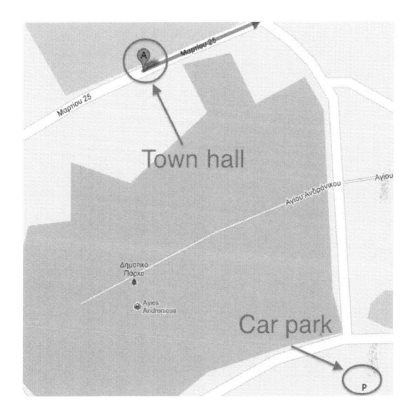

Opposite the parking area is the municipal park. It's not hard to miss!

## Ayiou Andronikos Church

Situated inside the park you will find a cute little church, Ayiou Andronikos, dating back to the 16th century. It's free to have a look around and houses some beautiful wall paintings of great religious importance. The wall paintings were covered up during the Ottoman rule, when the church was converted to a mosque, but were restored to their former glory in the late 1960s. Please note, the church is closed on Sunday.

## PART 2

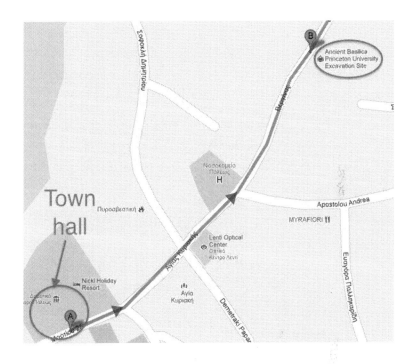

If you cross over the park you will find the town hall on the opposite side of the road. From this point, turn right and keep straight on this road. Eventually you will come to the Ancient Basilica excavation site on your right.

## Ancient Basilica Excavation Site

Excavations started in 1983 by Princeton University, in hopes of uncovering the ancient city of Marion/Arsinoe, and were completed in 2007. Some of the architectural remains discovered date back to 1000 BC and within the site; there is also evidence of a sanctuary to 'the Goddess' from around the sixth century.

There may not be too much to do here but I find it amazing to just stand and observe the history beneath your feet. Here you can marvel at the remains of this ancient palatial building and its surroundings.

## PART 3

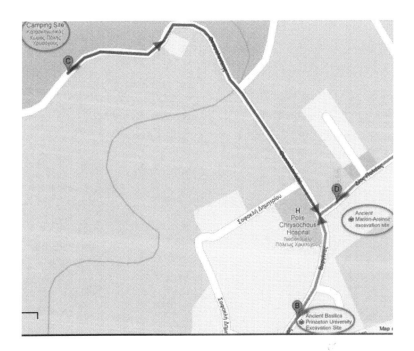

The next part of the walk takes around 10 minutes. On leaving the excavation site, turn right and make your way along the road, following it all the way round as it bends to the left.

You should see the hospital on your left. Carry on straight as the road bends to the left again.

Eventually you should see the camp site on your right.

## Polis Camp Site and Beach

The campsite itself is situated in a wooded area just by the beach and is a beautiful spot to sit and relax. There is also a snack bar which is open during peak season (April to September). The beach is a wonderful place to have a little dip or build a sandcastle or two! The campsite is currently being upgraded (as of the end of 2012) so an overnight stay may not be an option. However, this does not take away from the area's natural beauty and is well worth a look.

## PART 4

After a nice stroll along the beach, head back down the way you came and take your second left. The next point of interest is situated on your left (see the map in PART 3).

### Ancient Marion/Arsinoe Excavation Site

I know what you're thinking, 'Another excavation site?'. However, I think it's wonderful to fully explore the raw, natural beauty of these historical sites before heading onto your next stop, the Archaeological Museum.

## PART 5

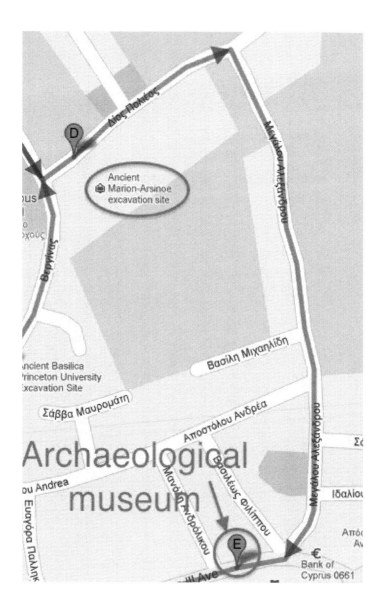

After leaving the excavation site, take your next right. Follow the road all the way to the end and then turn right at the fork in the road by the bank of Cyprus. The museum is situated on your left.

## Archaeological Museum

The museum consists of two major rooms with objects displayed in chronological order and which date back to hundreds of years BC.

There is an entrance fee of €1.70 but children under 14 can enter for free.

The museum is open from 8am every day but is closed on Sunday and Monday.

## PART 6

To round off the walking tour, you should now head to the market to peruse the local gifts and souvenirs. Turn left out of the museum and walk straight, passing over the crossroads. Eventually you should enter the market past the Elliniki bank at the end of the road.

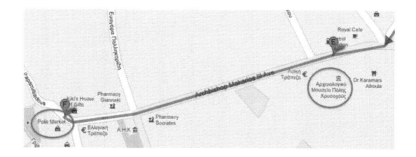

## Polis Market

Take your pick from the traditional handcrafts on sale or giggle at the funny postcards! This little market is less tacky than the one in Paphos and provides a lovely slice of retail therapy without being overbearing or garish.

From here you can walk all the way through to your next destination, Saddles Bar, for some much-earned grub!

# 12:00 pm -- Saddles Bar - Lunch

- **Price:** EUR €10.00 (for a single adult)
- **Duration:** 1 hour
- **Address:** 5 Polis Square, Paphos

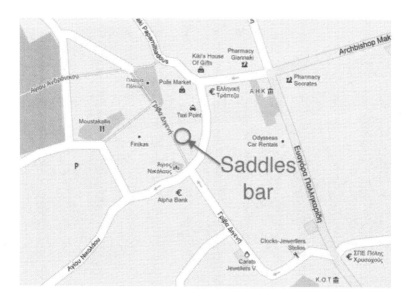

After wearing the soles of your shoes out, there is no better place to unwind and recharge than Saddles bar! You will receive the warmest of welcomes from Costa and Helen. Having worked in the service industry, both in South Africa and Cyprus, the Louca family know a thing or two about customer satisfaction!

*Local Tip: I recommend asking Helen for her recommendations for the food as sometimes there are tasty specials to indulge in!*

The bar is open 6 days a week (closed on Sundays) from 8am to 12am and offers a variety of yummy dishes from burgers and salads to pita pockets. There is also a pool table should you fancy a game!

Everything is reasonable priced with soft drinks setting you back €2 and coffees between €2-€3. Beers are priced at €2.50 for a pint and burgers are under €6.

There will probably be no need to book but here are the contact details:

**Tel:** (00357) 99 612 758

## 1:00 pm -- Saddles Bar to Ride in Cyprus

- **Price:** EUR €2.00 (for a single adult)
- **Duration:** 30 minutes

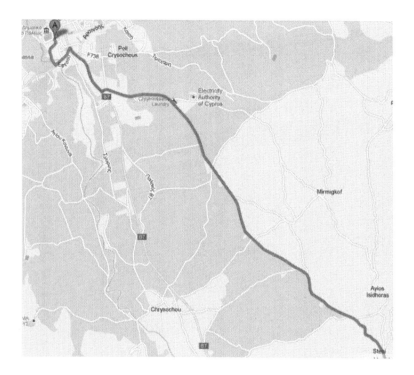

This journey is rather scenic and shouldn't take you more than half an hour.

Head back out of the old town the way you came in but instead of carrying on straight, take your 3rd left towards the Anassa hotel.

Continue on this road for around 6km, after which you should take the turning on your left towards Peristerona.

This road is rather windy but keep straight (keeping right at the first fork in the road).

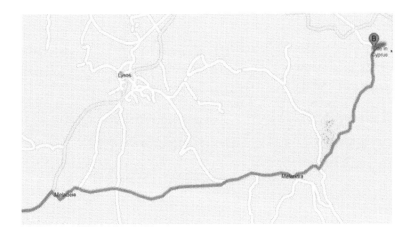

After around 2km, you will come to another fork in the road. Keep right and instead of going towards Lysos, take the road to Meladeia. There should be a lot of signs for the riding school by now. Keep straight, the road should gradually wind around to the left. Ride in Cyprus is situated on your right.

The fuel cost for this journey will be around €2.

# 1:30 pm -- Ride in Cyprus - Horse Trek

- **Price:** EUR €33.00 (for a single adult)
- **Duration:** 3 hours
- **Address:** Stavros tis Psokas Road, Lysos, Paphos

Horseback is a brilliant way to see the countryside surrounding Lysos. Ride in Cyprus is one of the most highly regarded riding schools and excursion organisers in Paphos and offers 1, 2, and 4-hour treks as well as day-long trips.

You must book in advance but the owners are lovely and will guide you through the booking process and help you decide on which trip is best for you.

A one-hour ride will cost €33 with a €5 deposit per person, a two-hour 'Sundowner' trek is €55 with a €10 deposit and a one-day ride (should you wish to go another day) is €100 with a €25. You let them know your experience level so they can tailor make your excursion for you. Please note, the 'Sundowner' trek will have to take place a little later to accommodate the sunset view.

You can book online or over the phone and you should try to do this about a week in advance, especially at peak season, as the horses are in high demand!

**Website:** www.rideincyprus.com

**Tel:** (00357) 99 777 624

**Email:** caroline@rideincyprus.com

## 5:00 pm -- Paradisos Hills - Dinner and Drinks

- **Price:** EUR €15.00 (for a single adult)
- **Duration:** 3 hours
- **Address:** Lysos, Paphos

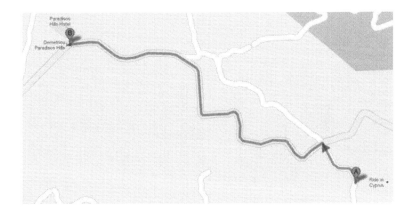

On leaving Ride in Cyprus, instead of going back the way you came in, continue along the main road, turn left and keep going towards Lysos. The Paradisos Hills hotel will be on your right. (If in doubt, you can always ask Caroline from the stables for directions!).

Please note, I've left some time between horse riding and dinner and drinks so as to allow time for you to get cleaned up. In the warmer months you can head to the hotel for a nice late afternoon swim and shower.

Set in the beautiful surroundings of Lysos village, Paradisos Hills is exactly what it sounds like - paradise! Relax in one of the secluded seating spots to enjoy the breathtaking views of the valley or (in the cooler months) relax inside by the roaring fire.

The hotel is owned by one large family who built upon the land left to them by their father. It is run by sisters Nikki and Soula who really do put their all into this traditional Cypriot Oasis. The outside area is wonderful with natural stone adorning the walls, brightly coloured flowers overhanging the walls and plenty of grass for kiddies (and adults alike!) to play around on! There is a lovely swimming pool should you fancy a dip and the rooms are brilliant value (around €60 to €100 a night for bed and breakfast), if you fancy spending a night or two in this peaceful little village.

The food is astounding and brilliant value for money. Don't expect to pay more than €15 for 2 courses. There is a lunch and dinner buffet most days from 12.30pm costing just €16 per person (with Sunday being the most celebrated day of the week) but in the winter months Nikki usually prepares the meals on request due to there being fewer customers.

There are also 1-day and 3-day cooking lessons available, where you can learn all about Cypriot cuisine.

For more information visit their website at www.paradisoshills.com.

**Tel:** (00357) 26 322 287

Truly the best way to end your 3 day Cypriot journey of discovery, now you know why I, and so many people like me, love to call this place our home.

# Things You Need to Know (Appendix)

## Transportation tips

### By Car -

While both the center of Paphos and the harbour are both rather small and accessible by foot, I would recommend hiring a car. Not only does this mean you can get up and go at your own convenience but prices are quite reasonable, especially off-season.

**CTT Car Rentals** offers cars from €10 a day with free airport delivery. There are also lots of car rental companies lining the harbour, all competing for customers so keep your eyes peeled for any promotions.

### Contact Details -
**Tel.** +357 99603751
**Email.** info@ctt-carhire.com

### By Bus -

Buses run every 40 minutes, daily tickets are available for €3 and are valid until 11 pm. Children under 12 travel for free and students can receive a 50% discount when a valid student card is shown. After 11 pm, a single fare costs €2.50. Weekly tickets are also available for €13 and bus stops are rather abundant in and around Paphos harbour and in town.

Buses generally run every 40 minutes except during the winter (December to March) the buses stop a lot earlier and many don't run after 3pm. To double check all routes and timetables, visit the website below or visit the large bus station by the main car park at Paphos Harbour.

**The Most Popular Bus Routes -**

Bus 611 - Paphos Harbour to Geroskipou Beach (Waterpark)
Bus 615 - Paphos Harbour to Coral Bay
Bus 610 - Paphos Harbour to City Center (Marketplace)
Bus 631 - Paphos Harbour to Petra to Romiou

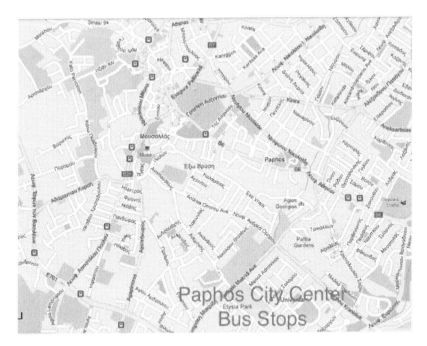

## Other Information -

For bus timetables - http://www.pafosbuses.com/

## By Taxi -

A Few Useful Taxi Numbers:

**Acropolis** - +357 26 951 584
**Chris Taxi Office** - +357 70 008 008
**Travel Express** - +357 26 923 800
**Daphni Taxi** - +357 26 952 096

## Food

**Etiquette** - There is very little to worry about concerning table etiquette in Cyprus. People adopt a very hands-on approach to food! Bear in mind, service charge is hardly ever included in the price of the meal and it is normal to leave a tip of 10-15%.

**Seafood -** When in Paphos, make sure you sample the seafood! The harbour is lined with fishing boats, all aiming to provide a daily array of fresh fish and squid. If venturing north, as recommended in the itinerary, Latchi is also renowned for its fresh seafood. I would definitely advise sampling the local Kalamari (deep-fried squid) a Mediterranean delicacy.

**Meze -** For those unfamiliar with this traditional style of Greek cuisine, a Meze is simply a small sample of food ranging from salad and vine leaves, to meat and rice. You can usually choose from a vegetarian, fish, meat or mixed Meze and these all come at a set price per person (usually around €15).

**Kebabs -**

Gyro: To put it quite simply, a Gyro (pronounced 'Gearo') is a Greek Kebab. In Greek, 'gyros' means 'turn'. The meat (usually pork) is placed on a spit, turned and sliced finely.

Souvlakia: This type of kebab is made by skewering chunks of meat (chicken, pork or beef) and cooking over a BBQ or grilled. The word 'souvla' in Greek means 'skewer'.

**Dips -** In Cyprus, the dips usually come before the meal with the bread, especially in tavernas.

Tzatziki is possibly the most popular dip on the island. It is yoghurt based and flavoured with cucumber, salt and mint.

Taramasalata is a rather shocking pink colour and is made from salted and cured fish eggs. Do not let this put you off! It is full of flavour and a firm favourite of the locals.

Tahini is like hummus and has a similar texture. However, instead of being made from chickpeas it consists of ground sesame seeds.

## A Few Useful Websites -

http://www.cyprus-eating.com/ - For restaurant reviews and recommendations.

http://www.paphos.com/v/restaurants/ - A restaurant guide including local tavernas and cuisine.

## Climate and Time of Year

Luckily, Cyprus has one of the best climates in Europe. It's proximity to the Middle East means that rainfall is infrequent and temperatures are fairly high all year round. The only snowfall and cool temperatures are in the mountains, in the center of the island. However, when it does rain, it pours! Thunderstorms in autumn/winter are not unusual. Also, far from the dry heat of the Middle East, Cyprus, being an island, can be extremely humid in the summer months.

### Spring - March to May

Average Temperatures = 15°C - 29°C during the day, 6°C - 15°C during the night
Average Rainfall = 1-5 days a month

Other Information on Spring:

When travelling to Cyprus during the spring, you are essentially avoiding the most extreme weather. It can be rather cool in March (especially in the evening) but come May, the weather is summery and rather hot on average.

These are the months within which Easter falls and this Christian festival is celebrated extensively all across the island. The greeting of 'Christos Anesti' or 'Christ has risen' can be heard and decorations are up for months on end. Make sure, if you are on the island during Easter Sunday, you make your way to a monastery come midnight for a fantastic candle-lit procession.

For clothing, bring light layers and long trousers for the evening as well as short sleeved tops and shorts/skirts for the hotter days.

### Summer - June to August

Average Temperatures = 29°C - 36°C during the day, 19°C - 25°C during the night
Average Rainfall = 0 days a month

Other Information on Summer:

In summer, the only place to be is the beach! Mainly because it is extremely hot and one of the only ways to cool down is with a dip in the sea. Air-conditioning is a necessity and I would recommend staying out of the sun between midday and 3pm. Everything is a little bit busier during the height of this season so booking ahead for excursions and restaurants is a must. Humidity is generally rather high throughout the summer, hitting its peak come the end of July.

As far as clothing is concerned, less is definitely more! If travelling in June, bring a few light cardigans/jumpers in case it gets cooler in the evening but overall, you will live in short sleeves, swimwear and shorts!

*Autumn - September to November*

Average Temperatures = 17°C - 32°C during the day, 10°C - 19°C during the night
Average Rainfall = 0-3 days a month

Other Information on Autumn:

Slightly less busy than summer, autumn is a lovely time of year in Cyprus. The sea is still warm enough to swim in October (or even November depending on your disposition!). September is still classed as summer in Cyprus but is not as humid or extensively hot as July or August.

It does sometimes rain in October/November so bring light waterproofs just in case. However, similar to spring, the pleasant nature of the season means you needn't bring coats or thick layers. Light layers, long trousers and closed-toe shoes should be packed as a precaution.

**Winter - December to February**

Average Temperatures = 12°C - 18°C during the day, 4°C - 8°C during the night
Average Rainfall = 3-6 days a month

Other Information on Winter:

Winter is off-season so most hotels and day trips greatly reduce their prices. Opening hours for many sights are reduced and many bars and restaurants close altogether until the spring kicks in. If there is something in particular you had your heart set on doing whilst in Cyprus in winter, it is best to double check times and availability ahead of schedule.

Even though the weather is cooler and the attractions less busy, this is possibly the best time of year to mingle with the locals as the coffee shops and restaurants suit themselves to accommodate those who live in Cyprus, seeing as most of the winter customers lies here.

Christmas and New Year are widely celebrated in this extremely religious country and the twinkling lights set up all over town are simply magical. The phrase ringing in everyone's ears is 'cronia polla' or 'many years', which is used for birthdays, New Year and sometimes Christmas. The Cypriot version of Merry Christmas is 'kales yiortes' which is the same as saying 'happy holidays'.

Make sure you head up to Troodos to see the snowy mountains and take part in some winter sports.

Often the favourite season for many locals, winter is the only season that allows boots and coats to be worn! Swimwear is really not an option unless you are thick skinned! Long trousers and jumpers are a must but some days will be clear and warm so don't be afraid to pack some t-shirts.

## Useful local phrases

Although almost everyone in Cyprus speaks English, it is thoroughly appreciated when tourists attempt to speak Greek. Also, in order to truly 'live like a local', you have to try the lingo!

Here are a few useful **phrases** to help you on your way...

- Γειά σου; (Ya su) - Hello/Goodbye
- Ναί; (Nay) - Yes
- Οχι; (Ohee) - No
- γιατί; (Ya dee?) - Why?
- Τι κάνεις; (Ti kánis?) - How are you?

- Ευχαριστώ; (Efharistó) - Thank you
- Συγνώμη! (Sygnómi) - Sorry
- Παρακαλώ (Parakaló) - Please/You're welcome
- Μπορώ να έχω; (Boró na ého) - Can I have...?
- Μπορείς να με βοηθήσεις; (Borís na me voithísis) - Can you help me?
- Πολύ ωραίο; (Polí oraía) - Very nice
- Καλημέρα (Kaliméra) - Good morning
- Καλησπέρα (Kalispéra) - Good evening
- Στην υγειά μας! (Stin iyá mas!) - Cheers! (To our health)
- Δεν καταλαβαίνω (Then katalavéno) - I don't understand
- Μιλάτε αγγλικά; (Miláte angliká?) - Do you speak English?
- Πόσο κάνει αυτό; (Póso káni aftó?) - How much is this?
- Πού είναι η τουαλέτα; (Pou íne i twaléta?) - Where is the toilet?

## Numbers

- ένα; (Ena) - One
- δυο; (Dio) - Two
- τρία; (Tria) - Three
- τέσσερα; (Tessera) - Four
- πέντε; (Pendeh) - Five
- έξι; (Exi) - Six
- επτά; (Efta) - Seven
- οκτώ; (Octo) - Eight
- εννέα; (En eya) - Nine
- δέκα; (Deka) - Ten
- έντεκα; (Endeka) - Eleven
- δώδεκα; (Dodeka) - Twelve
- δεκατρία; (Deka tria) - Thirteen

- δεκατέσσερα; (Deka tessera) - Fourteen
- δεκαπέντε; (Deka pendeh) - Fifteen
- δεκαέξι; (Deka exi) - Sixteen
- δεκαεπτά; (Deka efta) - Seventeen
- δεκαοκτώ; (Deka octo) - Eighteen
- δεκαεννέα; (Deka en eya) - Nineteen
- είκοσι; (Ikosi) - Twenty

## Other ways to live like a local

The nightlife in Paphos was once concentrated to just one street in Kato Paphos (harbour area), Agiou Antoniou Street (or more affectionately known as 'Bar Street'). Now, however, most of the popular bars and clubs are situated in the city center rather than the Harbour.

Coffee shops are a local haunt for most people in Cyprus and don't be fooled by the genre of establishment! Coffee shops on the island serve a variety of beer, wine and cocktails as well as serving food.

There are still some hot-spots by the water, offering brilliant views and nice vibes but if you venture a little further inland you can find some great local places, which are wonderfully kept secrets compared to the more garish options for tourists.

Other than those mentioned in the itinerary, here are a few recommendations and what these other local haunts have to offer...

### Metaximas Cafe

Comfortable yet modern, this coffee shop is a real hit with the locals and is open until 2am. To get there, just walk up the road opposite the Almyra Hotel in the Harbour.

## Sunset Breeze Restaurant and Bar

Not only does this restaurant have a the most wonderful views but the chefs are Le Cordon Bleu certified and the owners, Alex and Maria, make every effort to make you feel welcome. There is a play area for children as well as colouring and games to keep them occupied!

Everything on the menu is fresh. Maria prides herself on having only one freezer (and that's for the home-made icecream!) The food is reasonably priced considering the work that goes into each creation and the quality of ingredients. Expect to pay around €10 - €15 per meal with the steak costing €18.

I highly recommend the Mojitos! All cocktails are only €5.50 each and are prepared by highly trained staff using fresh ingredients.

For reservations call: (00357)26940791

Visit their website for more information, testimonials and directions: http://www.sunsetbreeze.net

**Out of Africa**

By far the best fast food spot in town, Out of Africa is a wonderful little kebab shop situated on 'bar street'. Not only do they offer yummy kebabs, there is also a selection of crepes, salads, burgers and hot dogs. They also experiment with different sauces to create wonderful 'secret recipes'. The food is fresh and wonderfully prepared.

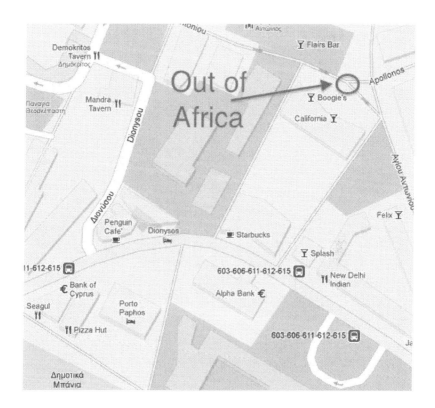

## Other Places to See

Obviously, living like a local is wonderful but the locals of
Paphos are already familiar with the beautiful tourist sites in
and around Paphos. For a little bit of culture, I'd recommend
the following possible day trips and activities...

### Baths of Aphrodite

This beauty spot is situated near Polis in Latchi. There is a
nature trail to walk along that leads to the actual baths, which
is simply beautiful and the surrounding area offers stunning
views. On a clear day you can see all the way to the Turkish

coast! There is also a wonderful little pebbly beach just a short walk down the cliff side. Legend has it that it was whilst bathing in these waters that Aphrodite met her lover Adonis who was hunting in the Akamas.

Opening Hours: 10am - 8pm

## Petra tou Romiou

Located on the road between Paphos and Limassol, this is said to be the birthplace of Aphrodite. It has been said that if you swim around the legendary rock you will be gifted with eternal youth.

Whether you believe in myths or not, this is a fantastic beach and swimming spot.

## Troodos/Kykkos Monastery

Kykkos monastery, established between the 11th and 12th Century, has been described as the most lavish in Cyprus. Although the original building was ravaged by fire, it was subsequently rebuilt and is still classed as the most important religious monument in Cyprus.

Troodos day trips are very popular and if you fancy a bit of the great outdoors, there is nowhere better on the island!

Opening Hours: 10am - 4pm (6pm from June to October)

Entrance Fee: €5

## Paphos Castle

A 13th Century Byzantine fort built to protect the harbour, it was dismantled by the Venetians in the 16th Century before being rebuilt by the Ottomans during the 18th Century.

A must-see for any history buff, the castle is a great activity to fill in a spare 30 minutes.

Opening Hours: 10am - 5pm (6pm in the summer)

Entrance Fee: €1

**Nicosia**

Nicosia (Lefkosia to locals) is the only divided capital city in the world after the Turkish invasion in 1974. There are a great deal of art galleries, museums and shopping areas to explore and the little cobble streets that weave around the center on the city's old town are simply magical.

**Paphos Archaeological Park**

Consisting of numerous historical sites from Prehistoric to Medieval times, this popular park is a UNESCO world heritage site. Points of interest include the Tomb of the Kings, The Odeon and Paphos lighthouse.

Opening Hours:

Winter hours (1st November - 31st March): 8.00 - 17.00
Spring hours (1st April - 31st May): 8.00 - 18.00
Summer hours (1st June - 31st August): 8.00 - 19.30
Autumn Hours (1st September - 31st October): 8.00 - 18.00

Entrance Fee: €3.40

## Other Websites

Here are a few useful websites to help you when deciding on day trips...

- http://www.georgesfunbus.com/
- http://www.amadeusholidays.co.uk/
- http://www.argonaftis.com/en
- http://www.prestigetravelcyprus.com/excursions.htm

Should you wish to find out any further information you can contact me here: bedfordellie@gmail.com

Happy travels!

# About the Author

# Ellie Bedford

I am an artist, English teacher, writer and wanderer originally from Cheshire, England. I moved to Cyprus at the age of 14 and fell in love with the Mediterranean.

I am now based in Paphos and wish to steer tourists away from the obvious spots and encourage them to see the real Island of love, just as we locals do!

# Unanchor

## Chief Itinerary Coordinator

# Unanchor wants your opinion.

Your next travel adventure starts now. A simple review on Amazon will grant you and a travel buddy, friend, or human of your choosing any of the wonderful Unanchor digital itineraries for free.

**What a deal!**

**Leave a review:**

- http://www.amazon.com/unanchor

**Collect your guides**

- Send an email to reviews@unanchor.com with a link to your review.
- Wait with bated breath.
- Receive your new travel adventure in your inbox!

# Other Unanchor Itineraries
## Africa

- One Day in Africa - A Guide to Tangier
- Johannesburg/Pretoria: A 4-Day South Africa Tour Itinerary
- Cape Town - What not to miss on a 4-day first-timers' itinerary

## Asia

- Beijing Must Sees, Must Dos, Must Eats - 3-Day Tour Itinerary
- 2 Days in Shanghai: A Budget-Conscious Peek at Modern China
- Shanghai 3-Day Tour Itinerary
- Between the Skyscrapers - Hong Kong 3-Day Discovery Tour
- 3-Day Budget Delhi Itinerary
- Delhi in 3 Days - A Journey Through Time
- 3 Days Highlights of Mumbai
- A 3-Day Tryst with 300-Year-Old Kolkata
- Kolkata (Calcutta): 2 Days of Highlights
- Art and Culture in Ubud, Bali – 1-Day Highlights
- Go with the Sun to Borobudur & Prambanan in 1 Day
- Nozawa Onsen's Winter Secrets - A 3-Day Tour
- Tour Narita During an Airport Layover
- 3-Day Highlights of Tokyo
- 3 Days in the Vibrant City of Seoul and the Serene Countryside of Gapyeong

- Manila on a Budget: 2-Day Itinerary
- A 3-Day Thrilla in Manila then Flee to the Sea
- The Very Best of Moscow in 3 Days
- Saint Petersburg in Three Days
- Family Friendly Singapore - 3 Days in the Lion City
- The Affordable Side of Singapore: A 4-Day Itinerary
- A First Timer's Guide to 3 Days in the City that Barely Sleeps - Singapore
- Singapore: 3 Fun-Filled Days on this Tiny Island
- The Two Worlds of Kaohsiung in 5 Days
- 72 Hours in Taipei: The All-rounder
- The Ins and Outs of Bangkok: A 3-Day Guide
- Girls' Weekend in Bangkok: Shop, Spa, Savour, Swoon
- Saigon 3-Day Beyond the Guidebook Itinerary

# Central America

- Your Chiapas Adventure: San Cristobal de las Casas and Palenque, Mexico 5-Day Itinerary
- Mexico City 3-Day Highlights Itinerary
- Everything to see or do in Mexico City - 7-Day Itinerary
- Todo lo que hay que ver o hacer en la Ciudad de México - Itinerario de 7 Días
- Cancun and Mayan Riviera 5-Day Itinerary (3rd Edition)

# Europe

## France

- Paris to Chartres Cathedral: 1-Day Tour Itinerary
- A 3-Day Tour of Mont St Michel, Normandy and Brittany
- Paris 4-Day Winter Wonderland
- The Best of Paris in One Day
- Paris 1-Day Itinerary - Streets of Montmartre
- Paris 3-Day Walking Tour: See Paris Like a Local
- Paris for Free: 3 Days
- Art Lovers' Paris: A 2-Day Artistic Tour of the City of Lights

## Italy

- Discover Rome's Layers: A 3-Day Walking Tour
- A 3-Day Tour Around Ancient Rome
- 3 Days of Roman Adventure: spending time and money efficiently in Rome
- A Day on Lake Como, Italy
- Milan Unknown - A 3-day tour itinerary
- Landscape, Food, & Trulli: 1 Week in Puglia, the Valle d'Itria, and Matera
- 3-Day Florence Walking Tours
- Florence, Italy 3-Day Art & Culture Itinerary
- See Siena in a Day
- Three Romantic Walks in Venice

# Spain

- Málaga, Spain – 2-Day Tour from the Moors to Picasso
- Mijas - One Day Tour of an Andalucían White Village
- Two-Day Tour in Sunny Seville, Spain
- FC Barcelona: More than a Club (A 1-Day Experience)
- 3-Day Highlights of Barcelona Itinerary
- Ibiza on a Budget - Three-Day Itinerary
- Three days exploring Logroño and La Rioja by public transport
- Best of Valencia 2-Day Guide

# United Kingdom
## England
London

- 3-Day London Tour for Olympic Visitors
- London's Historic City Wall Walk (1-2 days)
- London 1-Day Literary Highlights
- The 007 James Bond Day Tour of London
- An Insider's Guide to the Best of London in 3 Days
- Done London? A 3-day itinerary for off the beaten track
North Norfolk
- London's South Bank - Off the Beaten Track 1-Day Tour
- Low-Cost, Luxury London - 3-Day Itinerary
- London for Free :: Three-Day Tour
- London's Villages - A 3-day itinerary exploring Hampstead, Marylebone and Notting Hill

## Rest of the UK

- Bath: An Exploring Guide - 2-Day Itinerary
- 2-Day Brighton Best-of Walks & Activities
- Bristol in 2 Days: A Local's Guide
- MADchester - A Local's 3-Day Guide To Manchester
- One Day in Margate, UK on a Budget
- History, Culture, and Craic: 3 Days in Belfast, Ireland
- The Best of Edinburgh: A 3-Day Journey from Tourist to Local
- Two-Day Self-Guided Walks - Cardiff

# Rest of Europe

- 3 Days in Brussels - The grand sites via the path less trodden
- Zagreb For Art Lovers: A Three-Day Itinerary
- 3-Day Prague Beer Pilgrimage
- Best of Prague - 3-Day Itinerary
- 3 Days in Helsinki
- Weekend Break: Tbilisi - Crown Jewel of the Caucasus
- 2 Days In Berlin On A Budget
- A 3-Day Guide to Berlin, Germany
- Athens 3-Day Highlights Tour Itinerary
- Chania & Sfakia, Greece & Great Day Trips Nearby (5-Day Itinerary)
- Day Trip From Thessaloniki to Kassandra Peninsula, Halkidiki, Greece
- 2-Day Beach Tour: Travel like a Local in Sithonia Peninsula, Halkidiki, Greece
- Thessaloniki, Greece - 3-Day Highlights Itinerary
- 3 Days in Dublin City - City Highlights, While Eating & Drinking Like a Local

- Amsterdam 3-Day Alternative Tour: Not just the Red Light District
- Amsterdam Made Easy: A 3-Day Guide
- Two-day tour of Utrecht: the smaller, less touristy Amsterdam!
- Krakow: Three-Day Tour of Poland's Cultural Capital
- Best of Warsaw 2-Day Itinerary
- Lisbon in 3 Days: Budget Itinerary
- Braşov - Feel the Pulse of Transylvania in 3 Days
- Lausanne 1-Day Tour Itinerary

# Middle East

- Adventure Around Amman: A 2-Day Itinerary
- Amman 2-Day Cultural Tour
- 3 Days as an Istanbulite: An Istanbul Itinerary
- Between the East and the West, a 3-Day Istanbul Itinerary

# North America

## United States

### California

- Orange County 3-Day Budget Itinerary
- Beverly Hills, Los Angeles - 1-Day Tour
- Los Angeles On A Budget - 4-Day Tour Itinerary
- Los Angeles 4-Day Itinerary (partly using Red Tour Bus)
- Downtown Los Angeles 1-Day Walking Tour
- Sunset Strip, Los Angeles - 1-Day Walking Tour
- 2-Day Los Angeles Vegan and Vegetarian Foodie Itinerary
- Los Angeles Highlights 3-Day Itinerary
- Hollywood, Los Angeles - 1-Day Walking Tour

- Wine, Food, and Fun: 3 Days in Napa Valley
- Beyond the Vine: 2-Day Napa Tour
- Palm Springs, Joshua Tree & Salton Sea: A 3-Day Itinerary
- RVA Haunts, History, and Hospitality: Three Days in Richmond, Virginia
- Best of the Best: Three-Day San Diego Itinerary
- San Francisco Foodie Weekend Itinerary
- San Francisco 2-Day Highlights Itinerary
- The Tech Lover's 48-Hour Travel Guide to Silicon Valley & San Francisco
- Three Days in Central California's Wine Country

## New York

- Brooklyn, NY 2-Day Foodie Tour
- A Local's Guide to Montauk, New York in 2 Days - From the Ocean to the Hills
- Day Trip from New York City: Mountains, Falls, & a Funky Town
- Lower Key, Lower Cost: Lower Manhattan - 1-Day Itinerary
- Jewish New York in Two Days
- Hidden Bars of New York City's East Village & Lower East Side: A 2-Evening Itinerary
- New York City - First Timer's 2-Day Walking Tour
- New York Like A Native: Five Boroughs in Six Days
- 3-Day Amazing Asian Food Tour of New York City!
- New York City's Lower East Side, 1-Day Tour Itinerary
- Weekend Tour of Portland's Craft Breweries, Wineries, & Distilleries
- Day Trip from New York City: Heights of the Hudson Valley (Bridges and Ridges)

## Rest of the USA

- Alaska Starts Here - 3 Days in Seward
- Tucson: 3 Days at the Intersection of Mexico, Native America & the Old West
- The Best of Boulder, CO: A Three-Day Guide
- Louisville: Three Days in Derby City
- A Local's Guide to the Hamptons 3 Day Itinerary
- New Haven Highlights: Art, Culture & History 3-Day Itinerary
- 2 Days Exploring Haunted Key West
- 3-Day Discover Orlando Itinerary
- Three Days in the Sunshine City of St. Petersburg, Florida
- Atlanta 3-Day Highlights
- Savannah 3-Day Highlights Itinerary
- Lesser-known Oahu in 4 Days on a Budget
- Local's Guide to Oahu - 3-Day Tour Itinerary
- Tackling 10 Must-Dos on the Big Island in 3 Days
- Chicago Food, Art and Funky Neighborhoods in 3 Days
- 3-Day Chicago Highlights Itinerary
- Famous Art & Outstanding Restaurants in Chicago 1-Day Itinerary
- 6-Hour "Layover" Chicago
- Beer Lovers 3-Day Guide To Northern California
- The Best of Kansas City: 3-Day Itinerary
- Day Trek Along the Hudson River
- Wichita From Cowtown to Air Capital in 2 Days
- La Grange, Kentucky: A 3-Day Tour Itinerary
- Paris Foodie Classics: 1 Day of French Food
- New Orleans 3-Day Itinerary

- Weekend Day Trip from New York City: The Wine & Whiskey Trail
- Baltimore: A Harbor, Parks, History, Seafood & Art - 3-Day Itinerary
- Navigating Centuries of Boston's Nautical History in One Day
- Rainy Day Boston One-Day Itinerary
- Boston 2-Day Historic Highlights Itinerary
- Summer in Jackson Hole: Local Tips for the Perfect Three to Five Day Adventure
- Las Vegas - Gaming Destination Diversions - Ultimate 3-Day Itinerary
- Las Vegas on a Budget - 3-Day Itinerary
- Cruisin' Asbury like a Local in 1 Day
- Girls' 3-Day Weekend Summer Getaway in Asheville, NC
- Five Days in the Wild Outer Banks of North Carolina
- Family Weekend in Columbus, OH
- Ohio State Game Day Weekend
- Portland Bike and Bite: A 2-Day Itinerary
- Three Days Livin' as a True and Local Portlander
- A Laid-Back Long Weekend in Austin, TX
- 3 Day PA Dutch Country Highlights (Lancaster County, PA)
- Two Days in Philadelphia
- Pittsburgh: Three Days Off the Beaten Path
- Corpus Christi: The Insider Guide for a 4-Day Tour
- An Active 2-3 Days In Moab, Utah
- The Weekenders Guide To Burlington, Vermont
- Washington, DC in 4 Days
- Washington, DC: 3 Days Like a Local
- A Day on Bainbridge Island

## Canada

- Relax in Halifax for Two Days Like a Local
- The Best of Toronto - 2-Day Itinerary
- An Insider's Guide to Toronto: Explore the City Less Traveled in Three Days
- Toronto: A Multicultural Retreat (3-day itinerary)

# Oceania

## Australia

- Two Wheels and Pair of Cozzies: the Best of Newcastle in 3 Days
- A Weekend Snapshot of Sydney
- Sydney, Australia - 3-Day **Best Of** Itinerary
- The Blue Mountains: A weekend of nature, culture and history.
- Laneway Melbourne: A One-Day Walking Tour
- Magic of Melbourne 3-Day Tour
- A Weekend Snapshot of Melbourne
- An Afternoon & Evening in Melbourne's Best Hidden Bars
- Best of Perth's Most Beautiful Sights in 3 Days

## New Zealand

- Enjoy the Rebuild - Christchurch 2-Day Tour
- The Best of Wellington: 3-Day Itinerary

# South America

- An Insider's Guide to the Best of Buenos Aires in 3 Days
- Buenos Aires Best Kept Secrets: 2-Day Itinerary
- Sights & Sounds of São Paulo - 3-Day Itinerary
- A 1-Day Foodie's Dream Tour of Arequipa
- Arequipa - A 2-Day Itinerary for First-Time Visitors
- Cusco and the Sacred Valley - a five-day itinerary for a first-time visitor
- Little Known Lima 3-Day Tour

*Unanchor is a global family for travellers to experience the world with the heart of a local.*

Printed in Great Britain
by Amazon